GUIDE TO GROWING CITRUS IN CONTAINERS

TREY WATSON

www.leggcreekfarm.com
www.lazygardener.co

Printed in the United States of America.

ISBN: 978-0-9982272-5-2

Legg Creek Publishing
PO Box 43
Douglass, TX 75943

Contents

Introduction 1
Citrus Tree Basics 5
Types of Citrus Trees 7
Varieties for Containers 13
Cold Tolerant Citrus 15
The Citrus Tree Growth Cycle 19
Citrus Tree Pollination 22
Rootstocks 23
Pruning 25
Citrus Tree Propagation 27
Growing your own tree from seed 33
Citrus Tree Care 35
Harvesting 49
Sourcing Trees 61
Summary 63
Acknowledgments 65
About the Author 67

Introduction

I grow fruit trees for a living – nectarines, peaches, plums, apples, natives, and many others. Citrus, however, has been more or less a mystery to me for years. That's because citrus trees are so much different than deciduous, temperate fruit trees. With their thorns, picky weather preferences, and winter harvests, they are distinctly different from their temperate cousins. The part of East Texas where I live and grow trees has a humid sub-tropical climate, but we still get deep freezes every year and temperatures down into the teens on occasion. I've even had soil freeze here and stay frozen for a few days. Climatic conditions like that are fatal to citrus trees grown in the ground.

I have a friend who successfully grew a navel orange tree in the ground for five years here in East Texas. He harvested some tasty, juicy oranges. He had been blessed with milder than average temperatures, and as soon as the temperatures fell into the teens during one recent winter, the tree died. He tried to protect the tree with multiple layers of tarps and plastic, and he even used a light bulb for heat beneath the coverings, but the tree died back to the ground. The rootstock survived, but the tasty, edible oranges were gone.

So try as we might, we are not able to grow most citrus trees in the ground here in East Texas, or in most of North America and the rest of the non-tropical regions of the world. And that's where containers can be your friend. Container-grown citrus trees can produce a consistent crop for decades, even in the coldest area. Even if you live in any of the fine citrus-growing areas in the world, why not include a containerized citrus tree on your patio, balcony, or deck?.

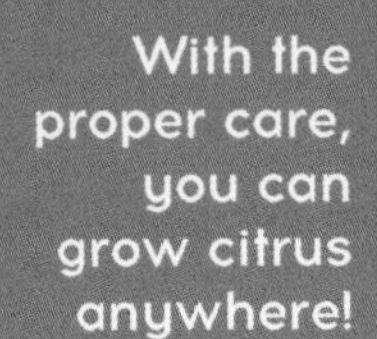

For the rest of us, the only way we can successfully grow a citrus tree long term and enjoy our own tree-fresh citrus fruit is to grow the tree in a container. I've successfully grown all types of citrus in containers, including lemons, limes, grapefruit, and kumquats. My hope is that this little book will help you do the same.

> *I can think of no better form of personal involvement in the cure of the environment than that of gardening.*
>
> — Wendell Berry

Places where citrus can be grown safely in the ground in the U.S.

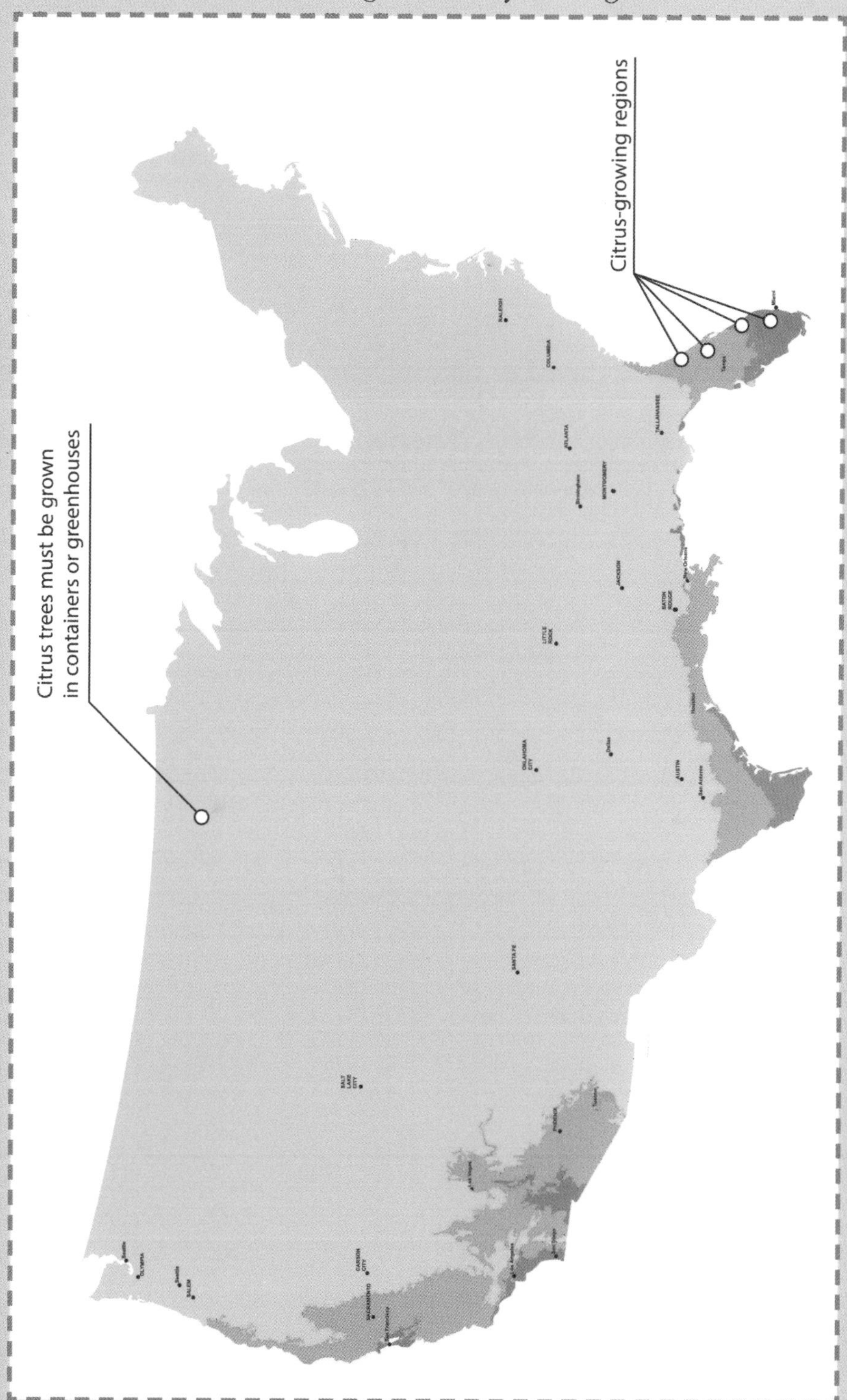

Citrus Tree Basics

Citrus is a genus of trees that has been cultivated for thousands of years. They are related to other similar species, including species of *Poncirus* and *Severinia*. The plants most likely originated from wild trees in Myanmar (Burma) and regions in the foothills of the Himalayan Mountains, though they have been widely hybridized and spread throughout the world since antiquity. The widespread distribution of *Citrus* and related trees means it's hard to pinpoint exactly where they originated. China, the Indian subcontinent, Japan, and Australia all contributed to the genetics that gave rise to the hundreds of unique citrus varieties we enjoy today.

Citrus has a long and complicated history.

Unlike temperate fruit trees, citrus trees do not require cold temperatures for the tree to produce fruit. An apple trees may need 600 hours below 45° Fahrenheit (F) during winter dormancy to produce fruit, but a citrus will suffer and die in deep cold. They do, however, benefit from some cooler temperatures during the winter. Some types of citrus trees benefit from temperatures down into the 30's (F). These temperatures can help with overall tree health and may also enhance the sugars of some citrus fruits. Citrus trees do have a "chilling" requirement, however; they need around 800 hours of temperatures below 68°F in order for the plants to bloom and produce fruit. In most cases these hours will be achieved over the winter. Citrus trees are evergreen, which means they do not naturally shed their leaves on an annual basis.

There are commercial citrus groves in almost every country in the tropical regions of the earth. The care of citrus trees grown in the soil isn't what this book is about. For those of us outside of tropical areas, our only option is to grow citrus trees in containers – or experiment with unique varieties that may survive some winter cold.

While citrus trees are almost always sensitive to cold, they also tend to suffer in extremely hot weather. Temperatures that remain in the mid-nineties for an extended period will tax the trees, though it will not harm them long term. Make sure the soil is kept moist during extremely hot weather. In some places, including at our farm, citrus trees benefit from some afternoon shade in extremely hot weather. I move our trees into places where larger trees will provide a little shade on hot summer afternoons. The temperatures here in East Texas regularly reach the mid and upper 90's during the summer months and I've produced consistent crops of citrus fruit – the trees just aren't happy about the temperatures!

Types of Citrus Trees

There are thousands of varieties of citrus trees spread across the world. Generally speaking, citrus trees are divided into 5 categories. Some may disagree with my categories here, but it's helpful to me if they're broken down as follows:

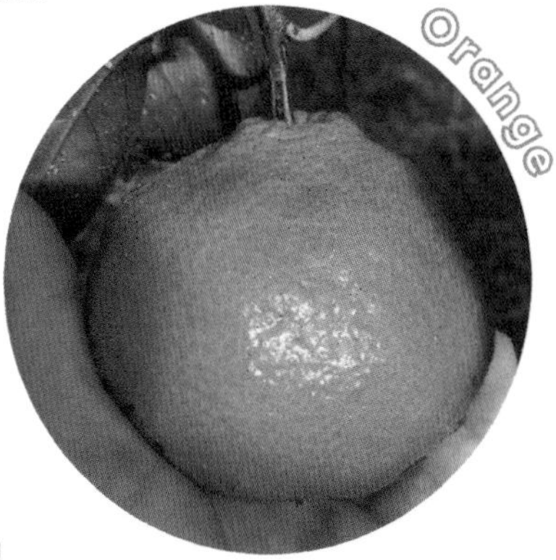

Oranges (and similar fruit) – This category includes oranges and orange hybrids that retain typical orange characteristics. Orange hybrids include satsumas, tangelos, tangerines, clementines, and many others. Trees commonly classified as orange trees also include blood oranges, mandarins, and sweet orange. The first sweet orange originated in China before the time of Christ. Historically, oranges were considered a dessert fruit. Orange trees grafted on standard rootstock grow to 20-30 feet tall if left unpruned. Orange trees can bear fruit for 50 or more years, including in containers if the trees are well-cared for. Orange trees benefit from a little cold weather in winter. Not heavy frosts, but occasional temperature dips to 32°F actually benefit the tree. In the 20th century, orange juice consumption became common in North America, and the orange became the most popular citrus fruit in the world. Orange

Orange

trees have some degree of frost resistance, which makes them ideal container trees. A type of bitter orange, the trifoliate orange, is the most common citrus rootstock.

Limes – True limes, such as Mexican lime and key lime, are the result of an ancient hybridization between native citrus trees from the Philippines and native citrus from what is now India. This hybrid was developed so long ago that no one knows for sure where the original lime was grown – only modern genetic technology allows us to know the origin of the limes parentage. Limes are used in a wide variety of ethnic cuisine across the world. Limes are usually green and round when ripe. Most modern species of lime are hybrids of true limes and other citrus fruit. Limes are fairly easy to grow in containers.

Lime

Lemons – Lemons are one of the most popular citrus fruits in the world. With a pH of around 2.2, lemon flesh is extremely acidic and sour, which means that lemons aren't usually eaten fresh. They are most often processed into drinks, such as lemonade. The flavor lemon juice imparts to certain foods is beloved around the world. Lemon juice acts as a short term preservative to fruits

Lemon

and other foods. Even the peel of lemons is useful in cooking as zest. Pectin, a type of sugar that is used to gel food products, is often derived from lemon peel. Lemons are easy to grow in containers but they are cold sensitive. Lemons probably originated in what is now India, but the plant has been widely distributed around the world for thousands of years. Lemons have been grown in the Mediterranean regions of the world for nearly 2000 years. Lemons and lemon juice have been used for centuries to add vitamin C to the diets of sailors and others to prevent scurvy. Eureka and Lisbon are common commercial varieties. The leaves of lemon trees can be used to make tea. Meyer lemons are small trees with some frost resistance and are a good option for the container gardener.

Kumquats - Kumquats look like dwarf oranges. They are one of the more cold hardy citrus fruits, making them ideal for container growing. The fruit is sweet, with a slightly sour center. The fruit is eaten fresh from the tree, skin and all. Kumquats are cold hardy, withstanding freezes down to 14° F, meaning kumquats can be grown in the ground in regions where other citrus trees won't normally survive. The tree itself is naturally semi-dwarf, growing to a height of 8-15 feet if left unpruned. Kumquats are native to south Asia, where they've been cultivated for hundreds of years. There are four cultivars of kumquats, each producing fruit with its own unique shape. The fruit often has a seed or two in it, but the tree does not

Kumquat

grow well from seed. It is usually grafted on a citrus rootstock, such as trifoliate orange.

Grapefruit - The largest of the citrus fruits, grapefruit is known for being sour or bitter. The grapefruit is the result of a chance hybridization of a pomelo, a citrus tree naturalized on islands in the Caribbean, and a sweet orange tree. The *grape* part of the name refers to the way the fruit hangs on the tree in clusters. The tree itself is not very cold hardy – it will sustain damage when exposed to temperatures just below freezing. The tree is also naturally large, so it must be heavily pruned to keep it small. Grapefruit can be grown in containers and the fruit is large and rewarding to grow. In the U.S., Texas and Florida produce many of the grapefruits that are grown commercially. Dwarf Ruby Red grapefruit is the best variety for container growing.

Grapefruit

Uncommon Citrus Fruits

The most common citrus (and related) fruits consumed in the United States are oranges, lemons, grapefruit, and limes. Other, less common fruit rarely seen in Western kitchens include citron, finger lime, Odichukuthi, Pompia, and many others. A few uncommon citrus fruits that can be grown in containers are listed below:

Yuzu – The yuzu is a small citrus fruit, native to China and Tibet, where it still grows. The tree is extremely thorny and tolerates freezes down to 15° F! It can be grown in the ground in regions where other edible citrus fruits cannot. Yuzu is a common ingredient in Japanese, Korean, and Chinese cuisine. Semi-dwarf varieties are best for containers.

Citron – Citron is a citrus fruit grown primarily for its thick peel. It's an ancient citrus fruit, contributing genetics to modern varieties of lemons and other citrus fruits. Citron fruit was probably referenced in the book of Leviticus (Lev. 23:40) in the Bible. It is widely used in Asian cuisine. Semi-dwarf citron trees, such as 'Buddha's Hand', are great options for containers.

Citron

Pomelo – Pomelo is a non-hybridized citrus fruit, native to south Asia. The fruit was introduced and naturalized on some Caribbean islands. The fruit is usually larger than a grapefruit and sweet, with a thick rind. The fruit is somewhat frost sensitive, but it adapts well to container growing. Thailand and Milo Mas are good container varieties.

Varieties for Containers

Any semi-dwarf or dwarf citrus tree, including varieties grafted onto dwarfing rootstock, is suitable for container growing. A few of the varieties we've had success with include Improved Meyers lemon, makrut (Keiffer) lime, Hamlin orange, dwarf key lime, and kumquats. Other good dwarf and semi-dwarf citrus trees for containers include:

- Dwarf Eureka Lemon
- Little Sweetie Mandarin
- Orlando Tangelo
- Dwarf Mexican Lime
- Dwarf Nippon Orangequat
- Dwarf Persian Lime
- Fukusha kumquat
- Tavares limequat
- Satsuma mandarin

Cold Tolerant Citrus

Certain types and varieties of citrus are more cold tolerant than others. The benefit of cold hardy citrus trees is that they require you to move them inside less frequently. They are more forgiving if you fail to bring them inside on a frosty night. Here are some of the more cold-tolerant citrus trees that work well in containers.

Trifoliate orange - The common citrus rootstock, trifoliate orange (*Citrus trifolita*) is one of the most cold hardy citrus trees. Trifoliate oranges are bitter and inedible, but the juice can be used in certain recipes and can be used for jams and marmalades. The juice and dried fruit are sometimes used in Eastern medicine. The fruit can be dried and used as a potpourri. The tree is hardy enough to be grown in the ground in many places. Trifoliate orange is hardy to -22° F (USDA zone 6)! Trifoliate orange imparts some cold hardiness to the citrus variety that is grafted on to it. One word of caution: if planted in the ground in the right location, trifoliate orange will spread by seed and try to escape cultivation, so be prepared to remove wandering plants so you don't end up with a thorny thicket.

Trifoliate

Meyer lemons – While not technically a "true" lemon (Meyer is a cross between a citron and a sweet mandarin orange hybrid), the fruit has the look and flavor of a true lemon, with less acid. It's one of the more cold hardy "lemon" varieties. We had our Improved Meyer lemon trees experience temperatures in the mid 20's on several occasions with no problems. They're easy to grow in pots, and they produce an outstanding lemonade or lemon cake. The tree is naturally dwarf. If you're new to citrus tree growing, try to find a Meyer lemon or an Improved Meyer lemon tree. They're forgiving and rewarding to grow.

Tangelos – Tangelos are a cross between tangerines and grapefruit. The fruit are sweet and the trees are hardy. 'Orlando' is a good variety for container growing. Tangelos are hardy to temperatures down to the mid-20's (F). Tangelos look similar to oranges and have a large amount of orange genetics, but they are mentioned here for their added cold hardiness.

Citrumelo – A cross between trifoliate orange and grapefruit, citrumelo is easier to grow in containers in temperate areas than a normal grapefruit. The fruit is very similar to grapefruit, but with better cold hardiness. Some varieties produce sweeter fruit than others; 'Dunstan' is the sweetest citrumelo. Other varieties are more bitter and sour.

Citrangequat – Citrangequats are a hybrid of 3 species – sweet orange, trifoliate orange, and kumquat. They are extremely hardy, withstanding temperatures down to 5°F. The fruit is usually considered inedible and the tree is sometimes used as a kumquat rootstock. It was developed in Florida in the early 1900s. The variety 'Thomasville' is often considered the most cold-hardy edible citrus fruit. It can survive temperatures down to 5° F!

Other great varieties and types of citrus trees for container growing in cooler areas are Hamlin orange, limequat, and some varieties of mandarins. Almost any citrus tree can be grown in a container with a little work, though dwarf trees tend to live much longer and require less care in containers than larger standard trees.

Star Ruby and Rio Red grapefruit varieties were created in the 1950's after scientists at Texas A&M University exposed grapefruit seeds to radiation and then planted them.

The Citrus Tree Growth Cycle

While they don't require winter chilling, container-grown citrus have their own unique cycle of growth. The blooming and fruiting time of each citrus tree is dependent on the citrus variety and the climate where the tree is grown. In commercial orchards, varieties are planted to have mature fruit at various times throughout the year, depending on the climate. But for home gardeners growing citrus in containers, citrus trees that bloom in spring and have ripe fruit in later summer,

New growth on an orange tree in summer

fall, or winter are best. If you're planning to grow citrus trees in tropical regions, then any citrus tree variety, including those that have fruit ripening in spring, should work. But for those of us who have winter temperatures that force us to bring our citrus trees into a protected area, it's best to select citrus trees with this growth cycle. The best citrus trees for growing in containers typically follow this same cycle of growth, with occasional deviations from it, such as fruit ripening earlier or blooms in late winter.

Spring bloom of citrus may start as early as mid-February, but we normally see it from mid-March into early May, depending on the outdoor temperatures. In most container-grown citrus, fewer than 50% of the blooms will turn into fruit. New branch growth also appears in spring. During the summer, additional branch growth will occur, and the fruit will get bigger. In fall and winter, vegetative growth normally stops, and the trees put their energy into ripening fruit.

The heaviest lemon ever measured weighed over 11 lbs!

The citrus tree growth cycle is illustrated here:

CONTAINER CITRUS TREE ANNUAL CYCLE

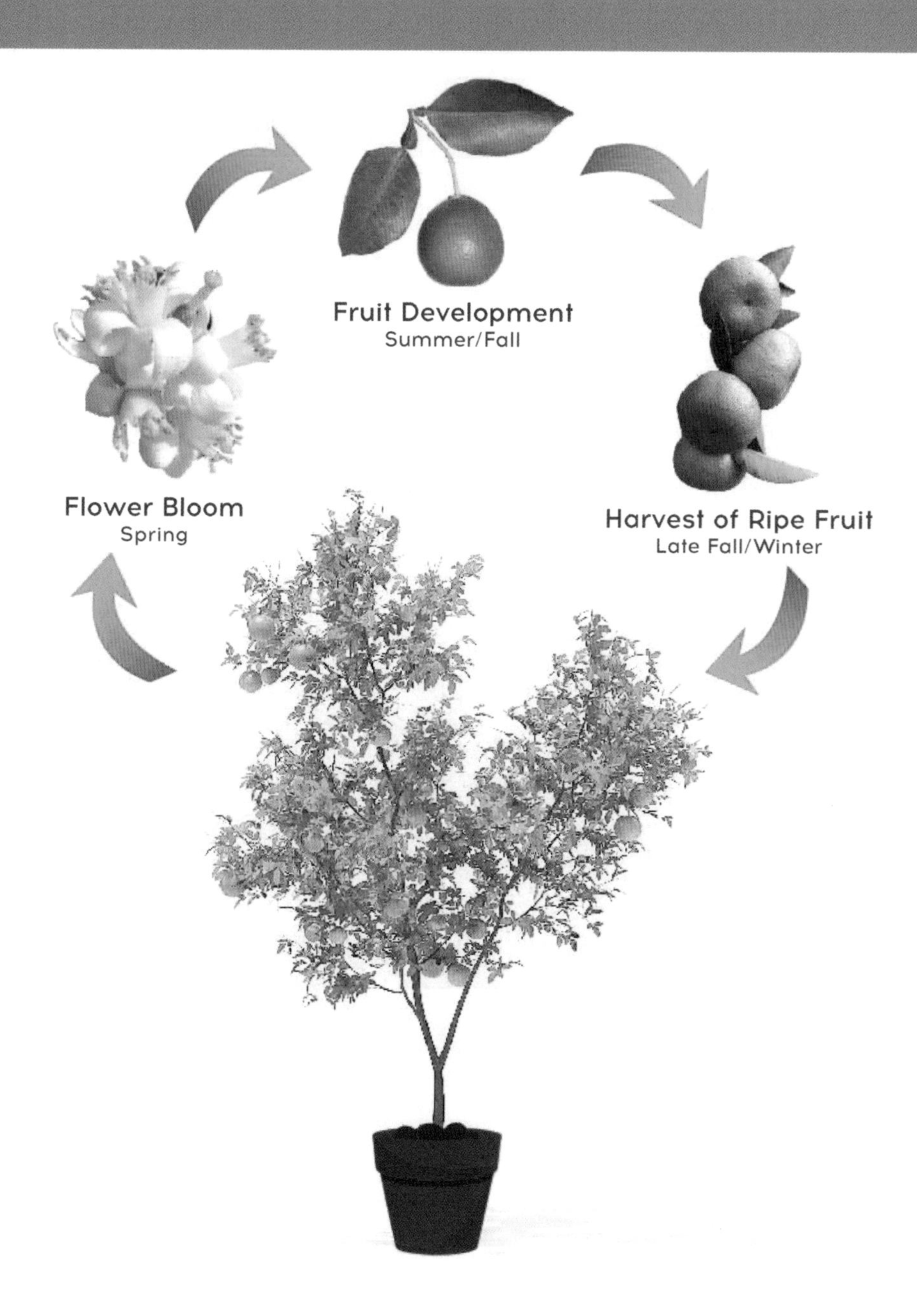

Citrus Tree Pollination

Most citrus trees will produce fruit without pollination from another tree. Tangerines and some mandarins are the exception to this – they require two different varieties for fruit production. In these trees, honey bees do the work of pollination. Many citrus varieties have parthenocarpy, which is a fancy way of saying they can produce fruit without pollination due to the structure of the flower. Seedless citrus fruit is produced on trees that don't require pollination. Some inadvertent pollination may occur through insects or wind, allowing normally seedless fruit to produce some seeds. Honey bees and other pollinators will still visit citrus flowers, even with citrus parthenocarpy. Many modern varieties of citrus produce seedless fruit.

A lemon blossom

Rootstocks

Due to extensive breeding, some types of citrus do not come "true to seed." This isn't necessarily a bad thing. Several years ago, I received a seed-grown citrus tree as a gift. It was grown from a grapefruit seed and it produced the sweetest, juiciest oranges I had ever tasted. Due to the genetic variability citrus trees and to increase the cold hardiness of the trees, most modern citrus trees are grafted onto a rootstock. Here in Texas, and in many other citrus-growing regions, our citrus trees are often grafted on the trifoliate orange (*Citrus trifoliata*). Trifoliate orange is a cold hardy citrus that produces small, bitter oranges. The trees are naturalized – and somewhat invasive – in some locations in

Trifoliate orange is a common citrus rootstock, thanks to its cold hardiness and vigor.

East Texas and in similar regions. They form a thicket of thorny trees. They have nice spring blooms and early autumn fruit, but they're tough to deal with when they get out of control. They were originally planted as a living fence for livestock.

The somewhat vigorous and cold hardy nature of trifoliate orange makes it a perfect citrus rootstock. There are other citrus rootstocks used in commercial orchards, but trifoliate orange is a perfect rootstock for citrus trees grown in containers. I've had citrus trees on trifoliate orange rootstock experience temperatures into the mid 20's over winter (near a house with the heat on) with no issues.

Trifoliate orange itself has been bred extensively and there are several varieties of this rootstock available. The variety 'Flying Dragon' is one of the most frequently-used dwarfing trifoliate orange rootstocks. A tree grafted on 'Flying Dragon' will grow to 5-6 feet at maturity, making a perfect container tree.

There are other dwarfing citrus rootstocks that work well too. Standard citrus trees, including trees grown on their own roots, such as citrus trees grown from seeds, grow to 15-20 feet in height if left unpruned. They can be pruned annually to keep them small enough for a container, though over time they will have the potential to outgrow the container. I keep several citrus trees grafted onto standard trifoliate orange rootstock. With a little pruning each year, they stay compact and happy in containers.

Pruning

Citrus trees grown in containers will often be limited in height simply because of the limited space for their roots to grow in the container. They can also be "topped" or trimmed to keep them the desired size, as long as there are plenty of lateral branches. Prune citrus trees in the fall or winter, after the current year's fruit crop has been harvested and before the trees bloom again in spring. Citrus trees do not need regular pruning in the same way as deciduous fruit trees. Prune off any dead or diseased limbs or any growth from below the rootstock throughout the year. Never prune a citrus tree back by more than 1/3 in a given year. Unless you're pruning to keep the tree small, you don't have to prune off healthy branches.

Alexander the Great probably carried lemons and limes to Europe from his conquests; Christopher Columbus brought some citrus with him on one of his voyages to North America.

Citrus Tree Propagation

In almost all cases, citrus trees are propagated by grafting a specific variety, such as Meyer lemon, onto a rootstock such as trifoliate orange. Like many other fruit trees, citrus trees can be propagated by cutting. The problem with this, however, is that most citrus varieties were developed for their fruit characteristics, not their longevity and toughness in the soil. For this reason, most varieties of citrus grown on their own roots are short-lived. This is the case across the board with fruit trees, with the exception of pomegranates and figs, which grow on their own roots.

Citrus rootstock, such as trifoliate orange, may also be propagated by cutting. In many citrus tree nurseries, citrus trees are grafted and rooted at the same time, effectively reducing the labor and time needed to create new trees. You can do this at home following these steps:

1. Have a good, healthy citrus fruit tree of a known variety, or have access to one.

2. In spring, after temperatures have warmed up and the days are consistently no cooler than 70° F, remove a 5-6" branch tip from the citrus tree that you own. The cutting should be ¼ - ½ inch thick. Cut the base of the cutting at a 45° angle.

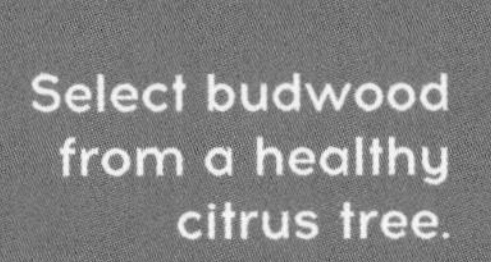

Select budwood from a healthy citrus tree.

3. Take a cutting from a trifoliate orange tree, making sure it's of similar size to the cutting mentioned in Step 2, with a 45° cut on the upper part of the cutting. Remove 50% of the trifoliate orange leaves (to reduce transpiration).

Take a cutting of trifoliate orange and trim away any thorns that may poke you.

4. Put the 45° angle of the named citrus variety on the 45° angle of the trifoliate orange, making sure the cambium (the inner bark) of the two cuttings are touching.

5. Wrap a small layer of grafting tape (available online) over the graft union. A wide rubber band, cut at one point, or some similar materials will also work. Apply the wrapping firmly but not so tight that the cuttings bend or otherwise warp. Be careful of the thorns! Don't hesitate to trim off the thorns.

Grafting tape, cuttings for grafting, and pruning tool.

6. Dip the lower end of the trifoliate orange into rooting hormone, available online or at some large retailers. We use Clonex brand rooting hormone.

7. Place the cutting, trifoliate orange side down, into a rooting medium made of about 50% peat moss or coconut coir and

50% perlite. If you don't have perlite, coconut coir can be used alone. Make sure the rooting medium is thoroughly moistened before the cuttings are placed in it.

8. Place the grafted cuttings in rooting medium. For best results, place them on a heated grow mat and mist them a few times a day, keeping them under a translucent plastic container. If you have one, a greenhouse with a mist system is ideal.

The lime cutting ready for grafting.

9. Give the cuttings around 14 hours of light per day. This can be from sunlight or a grow light or a combination of the two. Just don't let them cook in the sun! Filtered light is also good, so use the shade of larger trees or buildings outside.

10. Your cuttings should take root in a month or so. Keep misting them at least once or twice a day with a spray bottle.

11. Once roots develop, slowly acclimate the trees to outdoor conditions, exposing them to a few hours of outside weather per day (without the plastic cover) and increasing it until the trees are outside in the open air all day.

This is a relatively fast way to produce a large number of grafted citrus trees at one time. There are alternative grafting methods and grafting tools available online. Each of these methods, as long as they join the cambium of the rootstock to the cambium of the budwood, are viable methods for citrus grafting. To produce just the trifoliate orange rootstock, skip the grafting steps above and simply root the rootstock cutting. Trifoliate orange can also be easily propagated by seed.

There are numerous ways to graft and bud citrus; the internet is filled with helpful videos and websites showing the techniques, many of which can be done by the home gardener.

Growing your own tree from seed

It is possible to grow your own citrus tree from seed. Most deciduous fruit trees, such as apples, pears, and peaches, have such varied genetics that approximately 1-10% of seedlings will actually grow to produce edible fruit. Citrus trees, on the other hand, almost always produce a tree with edible fruit, and some types of citrus trees even come "true to seed," meaning they grow into the same variety as the tree they were taken from. Many varieties of citrus will not produce seed. Lemons, grapefruits, and some mandarins will produce seed. The biggest drawback to growing a citrus tree from seed is that it will not produce fruit until it is 6-10 years old! There is also a chance that the resulting tree makes fruit that isn't good to eat, or that won't grow well on its own roots. It is possible, but it requires an investment of time and patience. To grow citrus trees from seed, including trifoliate orange seeds for rootstock, try the following:

1. Select seed from a good, healthy fruit.

2. Don't let the seed dry out! The embryo will most likely die if it gets too dry. I like to use moist paper towels to keep the seeds damp.

3. Plant seeds about ½ inch deep in new potting soil that drains well. I've lost many citrus seedlings to "damping off," the fungal condition that occurs when soil isn't "sterile."

4. Moisten the potting soil and then cover the container with plastic wrap.

5. Place container in a location that gets about 6 hours of sunlight a day.

6. Remove the plastic wrap as soon as the seedling emerges.

7. Keep the soil moist but not too wet and make sure the seedling gets at least 6 hours of sunlight per day. You can also use a grow light to simulate the sun's light.

8. Change containers as the seedling grows larger.

9. Clean (sometimes called "sterile") potting media is essential for successful seedling growth.

Citrus Tree Care

Container selection

If you're an adventurous soul, you may grow your citrus tree from seed and after a decade (or maybe sooner!) be ready to plant it in a large container. Or, if you're like a lot of us, you'll purchase a grafted tree. Whichever method you use to obtain your citrus tree, the selection of a container is an important step. For the first container, select a container that is slightly larger than the current tree's root ball, or the container the tree was in when it was purchased. You do NOT have to put gravel in the bottom of the container. That will add weight and it will not really

Citrus trees can live for decades in containers if properly cared for.

help drainage. Adequate drainage is essential for successful fruit tree growth. Make sure there is at least one half inch hole in the bottom of the container. Some plant pots have holes in the center and around the edges of the bottom of the container – this is excellent for drainage. A citrus tree grown in a container with inadequate drainage will have disease problems and will eventually die.

Site Selection

Citrus trees are bred for tropical or near tropical weather, which means plenty of sunshine. For production, citrus trees need at least six hours of sunlight per day year-round. The advantage of container trees is that they can be moved with the seasons to allow for adequate sunlight. Six hours is really the minimum – 8 to 10 hours of sunlight will have a

Citrus trees are at home on decks and patios.

container citrus tree thriving. I keep the citrus trees with our other container trees, where they get full sunlight and filtered sunlight for 8 to 12 hours a day during the growing season. I also have some citrus trees on our deck, and as the seasons change we move them around to ensure they're getting adequate sunlight. I also make use of afternoon filtered shade. On intense, hot Texas summer afternoons, citrus trees don't mind a break from the bright sun. Using the shade of taller trees can help the trees stay healthy through hot summer afternoons. Just don't overuse shade – I only use it if the tree seems to be wilting even with adequate water.

Overwintering

The biggest issue with citrus trees and sunlight is winter. The winter for citrus is often the season of harvest. In our humid sub-tropical climate in East Texas, we are able to bring the citrus trees in for a few

Overwintering is the greatest challenge to the gardener when it comes to growing citrus in containers long term; get this part right, and you'll have a container citrus tree for years.

days at a time when it gets really cold. It does not harm citrus tree to go 2-4 days with inadequate light.

For gardeners in more northern latitudes, this can present problems, since it will often be deeply cold outside for much longer than a few days. A heated greenhouse, such as one that attaches to a house, is one way to successfully grow citrus in colder areas. Other greenhouse options, such as free standing heated greenhouses or even underground greenhouses are also ideal places to overwinter citrus in colder climates. I've used greenhouses to protect citrus trees, and even an unheated greenhouse works well if the temperature only dips into the mid-20's.

A sunroom is an ideal place for citrus trees to grow over a long winter. If you don't have a sunroom, a grow light is an option for longer term indoor citrus tree growth. Grow lights are manufactured to be on the specific light wavelengths needed for plant growth. They are usually available online or at some large retailers. If you have space, you can move your container citrus trees inside and use a grow light to simulate the sun's rays in a cold winter area. While different types of citrus trees react a little differently to indoor growth, about eight hours of LED light in a room that's warm enough not to freeze should be adequate for fruit production for up to a month or two during the winter.

Overwintering citrus trees is one of the biggest limiting factors to growing them anywhere. But bright heated sunrooms can allow for citrus tree growth indoors during winter. Grow lights of various types will also allow citrus trees to be grown indoors, even in a darker room. As long as citrus trees are protected from winter cold below the mid-20's and given adequate light, they will produce a consistent crop, even in colder winter areas.

Water Requirements

Mature citrus fruit tissue is at least 85% water. Keeping the citrus tree adequately watered without over-watering is essential to getting good fruit. If you leave your citrus tree outside the majority of the year, then you can usually rely on rainfall to take care of the tree at least some of the time. If you selected a well-drained container, then you should have no real problem with over-watering. We've received 6-8 inches of rain in a day, and the containers have allowed the soil to stay moist, but not with any standing water. If you see standing water after a heavy rain in your citrus tree pot, it is not adequately drained. A tree in a condition like this will die if it isn't repotted into a container with better drainage.

In the heat of summer, if it's dry with no rain, then we water our citrus trees every day or every other day depending on how the soil looks and feels about an inch below the surface. In a well-drained container, the tree will benefit from daily watering during the summer, from either rain or a water hose.

In the winter, when the fruit is ripening, it's best to keep the soil moist, but not wet. If you keep your trees outside all winter except during the coldest times, rainfall will often be helpful. I've grown several crops of container citrus with no supplemental water during the winter, thanks to frequent rainfall.

Citrus trees will completely defoliate when they experience drought conditions, such as if you forget to water them and it doesn't rain. If there's a crop of fruit on the tree, you will most likely lose it, but the tree itself will grow again once regular watering begins again, provided it hasn't been more than a week or two without water in hot weather.

Citrus Container Soil

Your citrus tree is going to be growing in a container for years, so selecting the right soil mix is important. Citrus trees aren't too selective when it comes to soil. The most important thing is that the soil is well drained. I personally like soil with larger pieces, and I've used the following blend with many trees that went on to produce tasty fruit:

- One part hardwood bark mulch
- One part organic compost (either homemade or store-bought)
- A shovelful of perlite or vermiculite
- Add a cup of organic fertilizer (optional)

Mix the above ingredients together and add to your container. The larger particles in the bark mulch make the container lighter and they

Soil mix for citrus trees grown in container (quarter shown for scale)

reduce the chance the soil will settle too tightly around the roots. It also allows water to drain from the container faster and it allows some aeration of the roots. I don't recommend native soils for citrus trees, and any soil that is based on sand will pack tightly in a container over time, restricting root growth.

Around 85% of all oranges grown commercially are used for juice.

Repotting Citrus Trees

Every few years, or perhaps more frequently, your container citrus tree will need a new home. You may choose to change the container once a year or once every other year, depending on the needs of the tree. I don't normally repot a tree until I see the citrus tree's fine, orange-colored roots crawling out of one of the drainage holes. At that point the tree is nearly "pot bound" and it needs a larger container. It doesn't have to be massively larger – just large enough to place the tree's root ball into comfortably without crowding.

A simple method of repotting a citrus tree is illustrated below:

Grip the tree firmly near the point where the soil contacts the trunk.

Remove the tree from the old pot by lifting up. If this doesn't work, lay the tree gently on its side and pull it out of the old pot.

Have the soil mix prepared to put into the new container. Put some soil mix into the bottom of the new container. Press the sides of the citrus tree roots in several places to loosen the soil around the roots. Place the tree in the new container.

Put soil around the new tree, gently packing it in with your hand. Don't plant the tree any deeper than it was in the old container.

Once the tree has soil around it in the new container, water it thoroughly. If the soil settles around it, add more soil.

Make sure to move your newly-potted tree to a growing location where it can be happy.

Fertilizing Container Citrus Trees

Container citrus trees need to be fertilized during the year. Organic, slow-release fertilizer is my favorite. There are a number of organic fertilizers specifically designed for citrus trees on the market – most of these will work fine. I like to mix in some organic fertilizer into the potting mix at planting. Compost, composted animal manure, or a purchased organic fertilizer all work for this purpose. Fertilize the tree around the trunk every other month with organic fertilizer – starting in early spring, as the tree is blooming and then every other month after that. If organic fertilizer isn't available, a balanced commercial fertilizer like 10-10-10, when applied to the base of the tree every other month works well. Apply 1 cup of fertilizer per year of age of the tree. I've also had success with slow-release fertilizers, such as Osmocote. Apply slow-release fertilizers twice a year – once when the tree is blooming in spring and then again in later summer as the fruit is maturing.

If you don't plan to fertilize with granular fertilizer, citrus trees also respond well to liquid fertilizers applied every other week. Once the fruit is mature and harvested, don't fertilize the tree again until it starts to bloom in spring.

Pests and Diseases

Citrus trees grown in the ground in tropical area orchards require a regular spray program. But container citrus trees, grown out of typical citrus growing areas, usually have fewer pests. Common garden pests, such as thrips, spider mites, aphids, and leaf rollers, can and will attack citrus trees. Insecticidal soap usually controls these pests. To make your own insecticidal soap, mix 2 tablespoons of dish soap in one gallon of water and coat all leaf surfaces with this mix. More serious, citrus-specific diseases can also bother container citrus trees. A few of these diseases are:

- Citrus scab – This disease is characterized by oval shaped lesions on leaves and fruit, growing to elevated yellow or pink spots on fruits and leaves. It's usually controlled with copper fungicide.
- Citrus black spot – As its name implies, black spots form on mature fruit, and immature fruit have oozing lesions. It's usually controlled with copper fungicide.
- Citrus melanose – This fungus causes brown spots on fruit and leaves. It's controlled by copper fungicide.

Copper fungicide is an old, tried and true organic method that controls fungal diseases on citrus and other fruit trees.

Harvesting

Most container grown citrus fruit is ripe in late fall or winter. Citrus fruit do not ripen off the tree. Oranges and similar fruits tend to get overripe if left on the tree for too long. Here's how to determine if citrus fruit is ripe:

Oranges (and similar fruits) – The fruit should be firm and fully colored. Most oranges are ripe in the fall or early winter, with the exception of Valencia oranges, which are ripe in mid-to-late summer. Oranges will become overripe on the tree. They should be harvested once the season is right and as soon as the fruit is firm, with the proper color. A soft orange is usually overripe or has been harmed by disease. A ripe orange should pull easily from the tree with a firm twist.

Lemons (including Meyers) – Lemons tend to keep fairly well on the tree. I've had ripe lemons stay on our container trees for about a month with no issues. Lemons are ripe when they're a bright yellow and the fruit is firm. Their ripening season is usually from late fall to early winter. Grip the ripe lemon and gently twist it off the tree.

Limes – Limes are ripe from late summer to late fall, depending on the variety. Limes are ripe when they have the characteristic green color and their specific variety's final shape. Some limes are wrinkly and weird looking when they're ripe; others are smooth-skinned – it all depends on the variety. Pull the ripe lime off the tree with a soft pull and twist.

Kumquats – Kumquats ripen from mid-summer to late winter, depending on the variety. There are only a handful of kumquat cultivars and each is ripe when the fruit is firm, with a bright orange color. Cut the fruit off the branches with garden snips or scissors for best results.

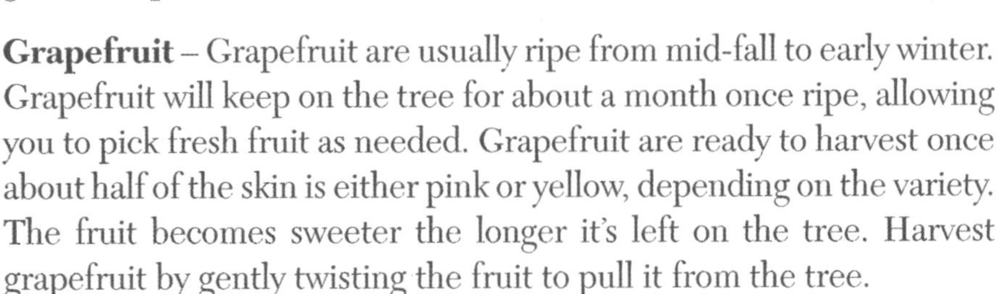

Grapefruit – Grapefruit are usually ripe from mid-fall to early winter. Grapefruit will keep on the tree for about a month once ripe, allowing you to pick fresh fruit as needed. Grapefruit are ready to harvest once about half of the skin is either pink or yellow, depending on the variety. The fruit becomes sweeter the longer it's left on the tree. Harvest grapefruit by gently twisting the fruit to pull it from the tree.

Storing the Harvest

Citrus fruits do not keep longer than a couple of days at room temperature. They keep for a few weeks in the refrigerator and they keep best in a drawer on the vegetable setting. It's better not to keep citrus fruit in a plastic bag, since this will hasten spoilage. Mesh bags are better – they will allow air circulation to the fruit, which, in combination with the cool temperatures of the fridge, will maximize the longevity of your freshly-harvested citrus fruit.

Many citrus fruits can be frozen. To freeze citrus fruits, wash and dry the entire fruit and place it into a zipper freezer bag or other freezer safe container. The fruit can also be halved or sliced before it's frozen. Keep the peel on the fruit when it's frozen, regardless of how the fruit is cut. Frozen citrus fruit will stay edible for about 6 months. Oranges may become bitter after several months in the freezer due to a specific chemical found in their juice.

A sliced fresh lemon.

Citrus fruit can also be dried, in both a dehydrator or in direct sunlight. The most nutrient-dense part of citrus fruit is the juice, and this is lost with dehydrating. Nevertheless, citrus fruit is sometimes dehydrated. Dried citrus fruit, including trifoliate orange, can be used as an ingredient in potpourri. Dried citrus fruit can also be added to bottles of water for flavor, used as decorations on baked goods, added to a cup of tea, or used as a garnish on a plate of food. To dry citrus fruit, slice the fruit into thin slices and place on a food dehydrator for 7-15 hours. Alternatively, place the sliced citrus fruit on a dark baking sheet in direct sunlight for 7-15 hours.

The peel of a citrus fruit can also be preserved. Finely shaved citrus peel is often called zest and can be made by using a zester to remove the outer peel in small pieces. Avoid removing the peel down to the white pith, which can be bitter. Zest can be dried on a plate at room temperature for about a day. It can also be placed in a food dehydrator at 130°F for 2-4 hours. Fully dried zest will keep for a year. The entire peel of citrus fruit can also be preserved by air drying in a low-humidity environment or by using a food dehydrator. Use a medium setting and the peel should be dry in 6-8 hours. Peel of citron, a citrus fruit grown almost exclusively for its thick peel, will take 8-12 hours to dry.

The most common way of preserving citrus fruit is by preserving the juice. Citrus juice is rich in vitamins and carbohydrates. Citrus juice, including juice from lemons, limes, and oranges, can be frozen. To get the most juice from your fruit, remove it from the refrigerator and allow the fruit to get to room temperature before juicing. Juice the fruit in whatever way you're accustomed to and pour the juice into ice cube trays for freezing. Once the cubes are frozen, they can be stored in freezer bags for up to a year. Fresh-squeezed citrus fruit juice will last about a week in the refrigerator.

Enjoying the Harvest

One of the greatest things about citrus fruits is the myriad of ways they can be enjoyed. Many fruits, such as oranges and their hybrids, can be eaten fresh. Lemons and limes are grown primarily for their juice, which is used for drinks and cooking. One of our favorite things to do with home-grown lemons is to make lemonade with them. For a great, easy fresh lemonade recipe, try this:

The Best Fresh-Squeezed Lemonade

Ingredients

- ☑ 1 ½ cups of fresh-squeezed lemon juice
- ☑ 1 cup of pure cane sugar
- ☑ 5 ¼ cups of filtered water

Instructions

1. Mix ingredients in large pitcher, stirring until sugar is dissolved. Chill lemonade before serving.

Lemon juice is also useful for adding to meal dishes, such as this lemon rosemary chicken:

Lemon Rosemary Chicken

Ingredients

- 2-3 fresh lemons sliced
- 2 or 3 boneless chicken breasts sliced around 1/2 inch thick
- flour mixed with salt, pepper, oregano, parsley, garlic powder (1/2 teaspoon each)
- 1/2 cup chicken broth
- olive oil
- plastic zip lock bag
- 1/4 of fresh lemon juice
- 1 or 2 fresh rosemary sprigs

Instructions

1. Preheat oven to 350°F oven. Place 1/2 cup of flour with seasoning in the plastic bag. Shake each piece of chicken into the flour mixture and fry in a heated pan of hot oil around 3 to 4 minutes on each side or until lightly browned. Drain on paper towels. Add to a pie plate.

2. Pour chicken broth and lemon juice into the bottom of the pie plate. Top with rosemary sprigs on each chicken piece and a slice of lemon on each piece. Bake uncovered for around 15 to 20 minutes making sure juices run clear when piercing the chicken in the thickest part. Before serving, twist the cooled lemon slices over the top of the chicken.

The leaves of lemon trees can also be used to make a tasty tea. The tea isn't caffeinated and it has a number of purported health benefits. To make lemon tea, select several healthy lemon leaves and wash them. Place them in boiling water for 2 minutes, then reduce heat and let the tea simmer in a covered pot for 10 minutes. Strain out the leaves and enjoy hot (but not too hot!), adding honey to taste. Lemon tea can be made year round. Lemon leaves are also used in certain types of ethnic cuisine.

Lime juice from home-grown limes can be used in recipes, squeezed over dishes, such as tacos, and used for household cleaning. Limes can also be used to make tasty desserts. To make a fantastic (and easy!) key lime pie, try this recipe:

Key Lime Pie

Ingredients

- ☑ One 9 inch graham cracker pie crust
- ☑ One 8 ounce package of cream cheese at room temperature
- ☑ One can (14 oz) of sweetened condensed milk
- ☑ ½ cup of fresh-squeezed lime juice (about 3 limes)
- ☑ One large egg
- ☑ ½ tsp of lime zest (zest from about 2 limes)
- ☑ 1 cup of whipped cream
- ☑ 1 lime for garnish (optional)

This homemade key lime pie tastes amazing!

Instructions

1. Preheat oven to 375° F.
2. In a large mixing bowl, whip cream cheese until fluffy. Add condensed milk, lime juice, egg, and lime zest. Whip until mixture is smooth with no lumps. Pour into pie crust.
3. Bake pie for 20-25 minutes in preheated oven. Don't let it brown. Allow pie to chill in the refrigerator for at least 2 hours.
4. Once chilled, top with whipped cream and serve chilled.

Lime juice can also be used to clean strong smells from hands after cooking.

A well-cared for lemon tree can live for decades; in tropical regions, healthy lemon trees can live for a 100 years.

Grapefruit is often eaten fresh, but this large fruit can also be used for cooking. Grapefruit slices are a tasty addition to salads and they can be used to make sweet drinks or desserts. For a great-tasting, easy grapefruit dessert, try a brown sugar broiled grapefruit:

Brown Sugar Broiled Grapefruit

Ingredients

- ☑ One grapefruit, halved
- ☑ 4 tsp of brown sugar, packed
- ☑ Whipped cream

Instructions

1. Preheat oven on broil. Place oven rack at top slot. Place slices of grapefruit on a broil-safe pan and sprinkle with brown sugar evenly. Broil for 5-10 minutes or until the edges brown. Remove from oven and cut out wedges with a knife. Serve at room temperature with whipped cream.

Kumquats are perfect fresh from the tree, but if you want to preserve some of their flavor, try this kumquat marmalade recipe:

Kumquat Marmalade

Ingredients

- ☑ 15-20 kumquats
- ☑ 2 oranges
- ☑ 2 lemons
- ☑ 9 cups of sugar
- ☑ 7 cups of water

Instructions

1. Finely slice the citrus fruit with the skin still on. Add water to fruit and keep in refrigerator overnight. Bring fruit mixture to a boil. Reduce heat and simmer until fruit is tender. Let cool and scoop out fruit by the cupful to determine how much is there. Add one cup of sugar for every cup of fruit. Boil the mixture of fruit and sugar, stirring occasionally, until the mixture begins to gel. Transfer to sterile jars and seal jars per manufacturer's instructions. Keep any unsealed jars in the refrigerator.

Other citrus fruits, such as Yuzu and citrons, have their own specific recipes, often with a regional or ethnic focus. I'm not going to pretend I know about cooking with those fruits, so I will leave the reader to search the internet and cookbooks for their uses.

Some container citrus trees will bloom during other times of the year when they encounter drought conditions. Some of these blooms will grow into fruit.

Sourcing Trees

Citrus trees are widely available in many places, both online and in certain large national retailers in the United States. Gardeners in the U.S. states of Arizona, Florida, California, and Texas must deal with state laws that limit citrus trees from coming in from out of state. Each of these states has a commercial citrus orchard industry, and these state laws are in effect to protect those commercial orchards from certain diseases that could be on citrus plants or budwood from outside the state. Other countries with commercial citrus industries, including Australia, also regulate the movement of citrus trees; please check with your own country or state office to see what regulations exist for moving citrus fruit, trees, and budwood.

Local nurseries often have citrus trees in late spring.

If you're in one of those 4 states, your options for obtaining citrus trees can be limited. Gardeners in the U.S. can try these sources of citrus trees:

Four Winds Growers
887 Casserly Rd Watsonville CA 95076
https://www.fourwindsgrowers.com/

— — — — — — —

Legg Creek Farm, LLC
PO Box 43
Douglass, TX 75943
www.leggcreekfarm.com

— — — — — — —

Greenfield Citrus
2558 E Lehi Road
Mesa, AZ
https://greenfieldcitrus.com/

— — — — — — —

Brite Leaf Citrus Nursery
480 CR 416 S
Lake Panasoffkee, FL 33538
https://www.briteleaf.com/

Large chain home improvement stores also carry citrus trees in season. Local nurseries are also a good source of citrus trees. Citrus trees are usually available starting in spring, when the danger of freezing temperatures has passed.

Summary

Citrus trees are fun to grow! Eating fresh oranges or drinking fresh-squeezed lemonade from your own home-grown lemons is tasty and rewarding. With the right variety, the right amount of sunlight, the right soil, correct watering, and correct fertilization, citrus fruit can be harvested from a container-grown tree anywhere.

In summary, you can grow citrus if you do the following:

1. Select a good tree from a reliable source (or try to propagate one on your own)

2. Make sure the tree stays happy in a well-drained container.

You can grow your own citrus fruit!

3. Use appropriate potting media in your container. Fertilize the tree once it starts blooming.

4. Keep the tree in a location where it gets 6+ hours of sunlight year round.

5. Protect the tree from freezing temperatures, moving it inside a greenhouse, sunroom, or a room with artificial lights (grow lights) when the temperatures drop. Short term (2-4 days) movement inside without much light shouldn't hurt the trees.

6. Keep the potting media (soil) moist throughout the growing season and through fruit harvest, which will most likely be in late fall or winter.

7. Keep the tree from drying out too much after harvest and prepare to start the process again once the weather warms up.

If you have any questions or comments on this book, feel free to email me at sales@leggcreekfarm.com. Check out the other books in the Lazy Gardener series. #LazyGardener #LeggCreekFarm

Thanks for reading and happy growing!

Acknowledgments

I'd like to thank all of you amazing readers who read my books – I couldn't do this without you. Thank you! I'd also like to thank my beautiful wife, who puts up with citrus trees in the house each winter and who provided kindly critical editing and proofreading, and who helped me with recipes. I'd also like to thank Ajmer Singh, my book designer, who always surprises me with his fresh designs that stand the test of time.

"....they will make gardens and eat their fruit."

Amos 9:14

About the Author

Trey Watson grew up in East Texas where he still lives with his family. Trey has a Bachelor's degree in Horticulture and a Master of Science degree in Environmental Science, both from Stephen F. Austin State University. He is a lifelong gardener and plant fanatic.

In addition to being an author, he is also the owner of Legg Creek Farm, LLC, a nursery specializing in fruit-bearing plants for the southeastern U.S. Trey is also the author of a children's book series called The Adventures of Mac The Fire Truck.

In his spare time, Trey enjoys hanging out with his family and exploring the outdoors.

Have a comment

or suggestion about this book?

Email me at sales@leggcreekfarm.com

I'd love to hear your lazy gardening idea or suggestion!

Trey Watson

Printed in Great Britain
by Amazon

61352985R00041